First Verses Known by Heart

Selected poems from the collections of

Susan Easton

With photographs by Erica Simone

Muffinworks Press
Burlingame, California
www.muffinworks.com

First Edition published September, 2007.

Designed by Erica Simone (www.ericasimone.com) and set in Scriptina and Arno Pro types.

Printed and bound in the United States of America.

Library of Congress Cataloging-in-Publication Data is on file with the Library of Congress.

Easton, Susan
First Verses Known By Heart: selected poems from the collections of / by Susan Easton
– 1st ed.
p. cm.
Includes index.
ISBN-13: 978-0-9749694-0-4 (paperback: alk. paper)
ISBN-10: 0-9749694-0-0 (paperback. alk. paper)

I. Title. [1. Poetry – Modern American. 2. Poems – Selections.]

Library of Congress Control Number: 2007905199

10 9 8 7 6 5 4 3 2 1

FIRST PRINTING

Muffinworks Press
Burlingame, California, 94010
www.muffinworks.com

A Dedication

My heart is often an open book,

Yellowing with the ages

Love is no secret, even kept,

Emotions mark the pages.

The Runic Alphabet:

ᚠ A	ᛝ J	ᚱ R
ᛒ B	ᚲ K	ᛋ S
ᛜ D	ᛚ L	ᛏ T
ᛗ E	ᛗ M	ᚾ U
ᚠ F	ᛇ N	ᚹ W
ᚷ G	ᛝ ng	ᛉ Z
ᚺ H	ᛟ O	
ᛁ I	ᛕ P	

     The Runic alphabets are a set of related alphabets using letters (known as runes), used to write Germanic languages before and shortly after the Christianization of Scandinavia and the British Isles. Runes were originated by the Scandinavian god Odin who was granted their mystical powers through his self-sacrifice. The myth of Odin was told in the heroic poem Hávamál (sayings of Har, the high one), which is both practical and metaphysical in content. It sets out a set of guidelines for wise living and survival. In it, runes are attributed with the power to raise the dead.

     Runes have long been associated with the mystic elements of life, and were adopted by the Celtic peoples who were so instrumental in keeping alive Christianity throughout the middle ages through their monastery copying and illustration of rare and nearly-lost texts and wisdom teachings. The various runes used to illustrate each of the poems associate their mystic power with the message of the heart and the soul of the poetry.

Contents

Contents

Contents

First Verses Known by Heart

Selected poems from the collections of

Susan Easton

Second Sight Parting

Seek out discerning fellow men,

To sort out life's conditions,

Drink from the common cup and share,

The answers to your questions,

Leave what you do behind your need,

To catch up on the growing,

And walk a short, unmeasured course,

The pavements graced unknowing.

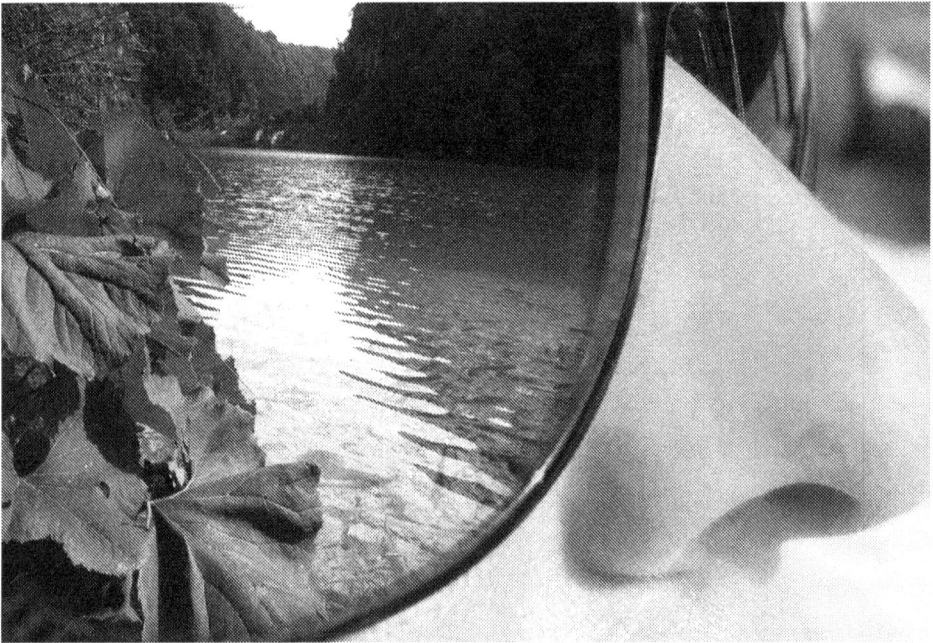

Sightseer

Once I was invisible

For all the world to see,

They looked right through,

And no one knew,

The vision that was me.

The Cycle Spins this Way Again, etc.

A baby cries......

Beneath my window life goes fleeting by

At some predestined pace,

The children play their timeless games,

And summer browns the freckled face,

Age turns the hair to silver strands,

As love wears thin gold wedding bands,

God hears the firstborn grandchild saying grace,

An old man dies......

Plainsong

Can I hold you close enough to feel,

What's going on inside me ?

It's something frightening and real,

And needs some understanding.

I'm all the things that make my life,

All visions great and small,

And here and now, I'm somewhere else,

Afraid that I might fall......

     from grace,

     into space,

     no place..........

     to put my anchor down.

Ode to . . .

Build not the walls that dare a scale,

The house without an open door,

The lock within that has no key,

A vacant heart with nought to store,

But further useless emptiness.

Paint not a rainbow hurriedly,

The clown without a laughing eye,

A still life of forgotten dreams,

A virgin singing lullabies,

Unto a secret cradle sweet.

Bend love into exotic shapes,

And friendship into abstract form,

With fingerpaints, feel tenderly,

For something endless, colored warm,

Be careful how you hold it then.

Underground Springs Prospect

I'm full of me,

In deep recesses, untapped,

Divined by rods,

The tree grows as the twig is bent.

For a Very Long Time

For a very long time,

There was a certain darkness struggling, groping,

To find the light.

There was a sun which only radiated to release

The pent up warmth,

But secretly, I felt a little chill of loneliness

Now and again.

For a very long time,

Busy was the best thing to be because

Having many things to think about

Staved off the one thought that haunted me,

There was a certain smile

That had no special place to live in someone's eyes.

But in private, I felt a smile eased the aching

Now and again.

They say there are things you never forget how to do,

But there are tributaries in the heart no ships traverse,

No one to book passage in your life,

Until, if you are lucky,

You see a face that fills you with hope

And you ask him aboard,

Quietly praying that this is the light and they warmth

that was missing,

For a very long time.

14

Love Sonnets

I shared myself before,
In progressive stages my concept of giving grew,
But with you my heart knew nothing and learned all.

Do you really know, my counterpart,
How it is to be inside your eyes,
Seeing me reflect,
Basking in warmth, naked,
Wrapped in joyous love.

I crawl into our bed and fall asleep,
While you are in the other room,
And have you just the same.

We came together
to ask and grant forgiveness
with our bodies,
Sleeping with only one cover
through the coldest night of our times,
When you come home today my love,
I promise to remember that it's spring.

I think about loving you,
Sometimes a chill runs down my spine,
I startle and stir awake,
To find you've taken all the covers again.

There's a different world beyond my window now,
Sunlight chasing thunderclouds,
After we've shared the sounds of rain.

Equinox

Yes,

I love you now,

As I did when knew you when,

And will til you're old,

And on and on,

As you are reduced to your immortality.

I've Come to Watch for Postmen Now

I took my morning walk with joy,
I breathed in lace and apricot,
I filled my pockets with the sky,
And left the door to home unlocked.

I turned the calendar ahead,
And emptied out the dusting drawers,
Of plasticized forget-me-nots,
That filled the garden of before.

I wrote a song about our love,
It sounded like a Christmas hymn,
I was the infant with no bed,
You were the manger they cradled me in.

No more chanting solitudes,
Putting up preserves and hopes,
I've come to watch for postmen now,
And peek inside the envelopes.

Lovelight

If I were time and you the sun,

The days would go on shining,

With youth as mistress of our nights,

Embracing in the endless light,

We'd hold the shadows out of sight,

Til sunrise heard us sighing.

Community Property

My house is neatly kept,

No dust or soiled linens,

Silver shines, the towels are fresh,

His, mine.

The cabinets are stocked,

We travel light, But move a lot,

Every dish comes with us,

But friends get left behind,

His, mine.

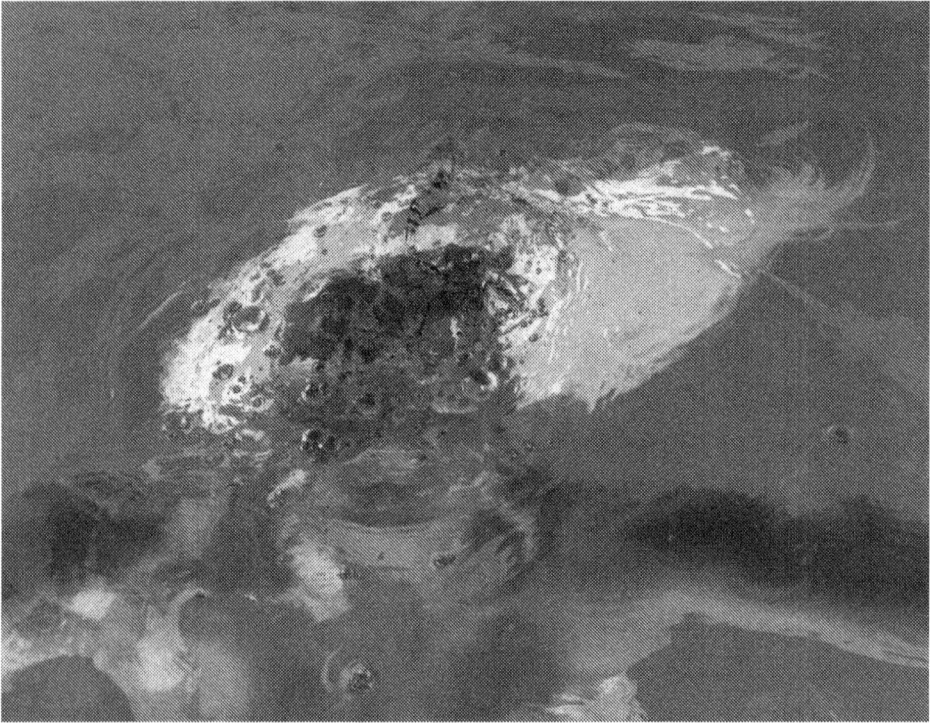

Open Heart Surgery

Loving him

Was like going under the knife,

Layer by layer

He sliced into my flesh.

Neatly, precisely

Clamping off the blood lines

Until...

He reached my heart

And delicately tried,

To replace the valves,

Worn out

By the stress and the strain

Of loving him.

Anti Plural Poem

I left my parent's fold,
Not very old,
To be your wife,
To have and hold,
Never an interlude to find,
Myself in the singular.

Five years behind and done,
Not very long,
To be a mate, to live as one,
Never a solo piece performed by
Myself in the singular.

I have died to be born,
Not very strong,
To be alone, to travel on,
Taking the time I need to know,
Myself in the singular.

Love and the Dow Jones Average

Love and the Dow Jones Average have a lot in common,

It is not unusual either

For love to run a course like the business cycle,

Macy's only has one big parade every Christmas,

But I have you all year long, so remember,

The customer is always right.

Love and a good meal have both been known to upset the stomach,

Why do you think they call it heartburn ?

Love is like an all American war.

If he sees the blue of a thing, she sees the gray,

Why do you think they call them civil ceremonies ?

Love is also like an unconditional surrender.

My Appomattox is just about the size of a double bed,

So every time you see me wave a white flag,

Drop everything and bury the hatchet.

Maybe then we can get together for a little peace.

Fancies

Our brief encounters collage into hellos and good-byes,

I gesture and you part a glance,

We touch while moments fly,

You belong to another world and sadly, so do I,

But fancy how we might have been together.

The words you've given to me form a scrapbook in my head,

Our scenes are few, but how I've memorized the things you've said,

The author let me glimpse the end, and nothing lies ahead,

But fancy how we could have left them laughing.

On Rocks

For every path I've ever walked,

I've known a stepping stone and stumbling block,

Two feet beneath, not always firmly under,

Wisdom is knowing when and where to wander.

"Nor Any More Heaven or Hell Than There Is Now."

(Inspired by a line from Walt Whitman)

Never any more,

The scales have always been in balance,

For every burial, a baptism,

For every lost love, hope.

Heaven and hell in equal weight,

Pulling against each other in constant tension,

Gravity that seals the planet like a Mason jar.

All is preserved,

Every dream, every disaster that ever was,

Never any more.

Funny Faces

Smile me once, laddie.

Everybody's cuttin' off their noses

To spite their faces,

So I'd like to remember your face before the hole.

Curb Feelers

Enlightenment came one day

While stringing watermelon seeds.

Someone said, "You're busy, but where will it get you?"

As if there was someplace to be.

Angels of Mercy

The paid dug in

Until she was visibly a gash,

So they wrapped her up

In Curad's ouchless bandaids.

Quote

Slices of history,

Verse and chapter,

Once we loved each other's laughter.

Watch When I Walk

Watch when I walk, without, within,

A skeleton strides beside my skin,

The peel is found inside the meat,

What once was bitter palates sweet.

Time is a farce and nothing settles,

Love is decided on flower petals,

Destiny wears a covered grin,

Skeleton, skeleton, please come in.

End Song

It's gone now,

Whatever it may have been,

That lit the eyes

Whenever he came in.

The lost chord,

Whatever the tune I play,

That echoed his voice,

Whenever he went away.

I miss it,

Whatever those times we knew,

That measured the love,

Whenever the heartaches grew,

It's over,

Whatever we've said and done,

That mirrored our joy,

Whenever we two were one.

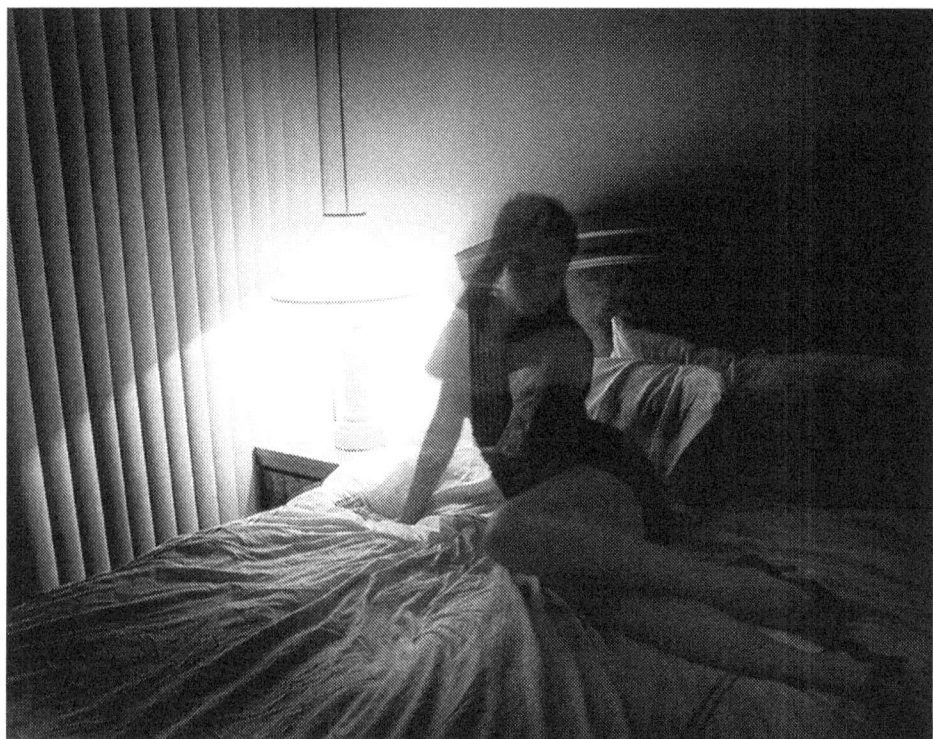

Bedtime Story

A wife sleeps in, but not around,

Unless the fancy takes her,

Night after night, a comfortable pal,

A teddy bear for papa.

Night after night,

Til the senses dull,

Patterned between the sheets,

A teaspoon of honey,

In ritual style,

Progressively less sweet.

Back to Some Dream

You inch along a single spot,
With fearful measured step,
The past is tied like apron strings,
Around the waste you kept.

The promised future is held out,
A tambourine in hand,
You beg tomorrow like some fierce
Salvation Army Band.

You count down days and rocket ships,
And tremble with each blast,
but manage still to miss the moon,
by running out of gas.

You set your star atop the tree,
The decorations glow,
So blinding that you cannot see,
The gifts that lay below.

She lives like Daylight Savings Time,
An hour up for light,
Beware the rising sun, my love,
Dreams do not stay past night.

Fare Thee Well

He found that very suddenly,
The world was his balloon,
The fates had blown him easterly,
On business for the moon,
Careening over mountain peaks,
An ocean bounds his mind,
She hoped that even in the sun,
He'd find his heart was blind.
How does it feel to be cast in the role,
Of some good knight fleeting past ?
While she in the tower your captive lies,
Holding her hopes to the last.

She wished him well with measured vowels,
She really wished him sight,
A greater guide than purchased tours,
An empty bed at night,
A million dollars for his thoughts,
The world to have him near,
While munching crackers with green cheese,
Pretending he could hear.
How does it feel to be bigger than life ?
Questioned a bread box below.
Someone had taught him goodbye very well.
She was hoping to teach him hello.

Laying the Ghosts to Rest

Inside the eerie mansions of my mind,

Ghosts of the past came haunting all the time,

There was no rest or peace, no stopping pain,

In unison the terrors screamed my name.

There is no simple way I can explain,

The moment that my freedom was regained,

But now I know the ghosts were ruled by me,

And only by my hand could I be free.

This poem is for myself and me alone,

It marks the grave of dragons that are gone,

The ghosts I hid behind are exorcised,

What's dead no longer hinder what's alive.

Like phantom pains, I still expect to feel,

The pity for myself which made me real,

But each day brings the chance to learn the new,

The seeds are history, I am what grew.

Afternoon Appointment

Called myself up,

Ask myself out,

Met myself there,

We went about,

Catching up themes,

Drying up tears,

Filling the void,

Left by the years,

Packing life in,

Putting grief down,

Buried the past,

Where it will never be found.

Abbreviated Epic

To love's a cry that rallies scores,

Desires march as off to war,

Ennobled spirits, banners furled,

All seek the spoils of kindred souls.

Some battle dress with armor plate,

While others cloak themselves in hate.

Some take the plains with nothing less,

Then uniforms of nakedness.

Blow comes to blow for those engaged,

Great hopes and expectations rage.

To victors come the conquered dreams,

The cause of passion is redeemed.

But oh the sad, barbaric cost,

Of hearts that went to war and lost.

Sometimes

Sometimes, sometimes you realize
That there is nothing to lose,
Because as philosophers say over breakfast
and in elevators,
We are all going to be dead a long time.
And suddenly you come to understand,
Zen Buddhism,
love,
and people who go over waterfalls in barrels.

Sometimes, sometimes in the middle of laughter,
There is a hint of tears,
Because as everyone is fond of observing,
Comedians only tell jokes to hide their pain,
And suddenly you come to understand,
One liners,
love,
and people who fall down to make you giggle.

Sometimes, sometimes we tremble
In the presence of those we care for,
Because everybody knows you can't stick needles in a pin cushion,
When it is wrapped in a box.
And suddenly you come to understand,
Acupuncture,
love,
and people who open their eyes so wide you can see their hearts.

Monetary Value

What did it buy you,

To covet gold and silver,

While under the sheets at home,

Love withered.

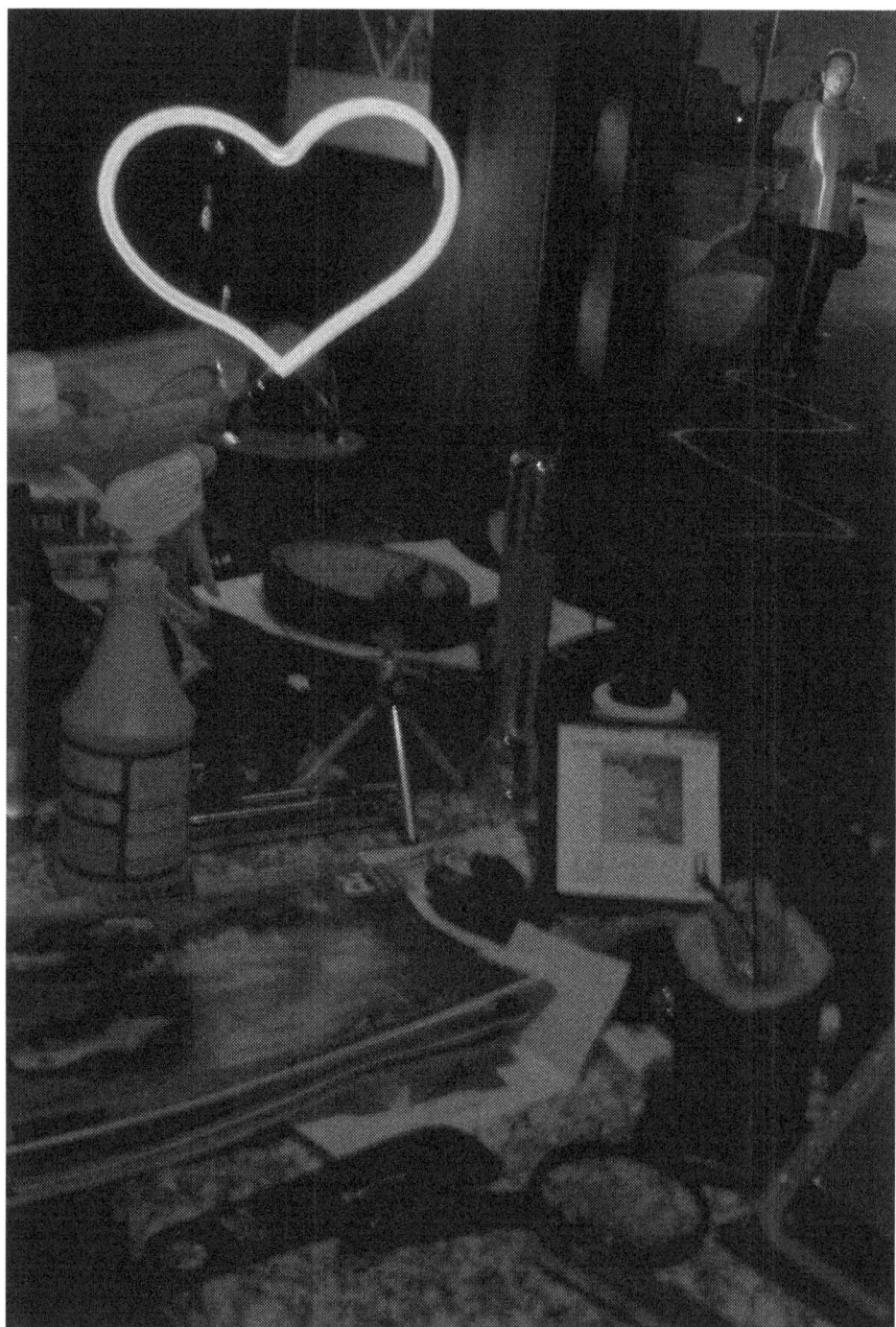

Over a Shoulder

The summer finally made her way to bed in late October,

And certain children of the light,

Who wished to have it over,

Call back to say that home is where their heart is,

To their wonder,

Now that the taste to wander,

Bitters in their empty mouths and lingers.

Offering Prayer

Were these the gentle doves chosen for sacrifice ?

Never a priest, nor death, could bring them back together.

Suffer these wayward children Lord,

Out of the fold. It's early in September.

Even the prophets failed to see the worst.

Remember the games,

The one they fancied winning ?

Dear God and Fermi, atoms and my friends are splitting !

Create in me a clean heart.

Blackout

Click

"Where is the light switch?"

Panicked bodies roll and tumble,

In the brush of linen jungles,

The faster ones with pretty lines,

And words that you can see through.

Click

"Where is the light switch?"

Anxious minds that would deceive all,

Show their illness, sex is febrile,

The hotter one with quicker hands,

And fingers that are clumsy.

Click

"Where is the light switch?"

Frenzied people tremble, then grope,

See the children jumping noose rope,

The bigger ones with longer necks,

And air that they can walk on.

Where When Why

Where did the Garden of Eden go,

When we let it slip right by,

Taking they only chance we had,

For a decent kind of life.

The smarter we get, the dumber we act,

The harder the way to see,

And now lies a city in civil war,

Where fond Eden used to be.

The Huckster

The huckster used to bring fresh fruit,

He cried like all street Arabs,

"Can-tell-lopes, water-melons, ripe bananas."

Crawling the alleys in his truck,

Making a buck,

Singing and selling in season.

Noonwine Kisses

I am taken back by the music,

Back to a day when time passed,

Between our mouths,

Pierced by our tongues,

Wet...

With a hint of sherry in the tasting

Seeing You Inside Out

I am part and parcel of the drama,

I am seeing you,

In the play within the play,

As the actress within the actress.

There are two of everything,

I wonder which is real.

I watch you from the audience.

There you are upstage,

In the costume of modern woman,

Saying her words as if they were yours.

Then I listen to the emptiness of every syllable,

I see you inside out.

I watch you from the wings.

I see the drama unfold.

Your character is sharply drawn,

She speaks and moves, then speaks and moves again,

Only to find the meaning of the journey lost,

Hiding fear beneath bravado, suddenly a self atheist.

I see you inside out.

I am part and parcel of the drama.

I am seeing you,

In the play within the play,

As the actress within the actress.

To the world you pretend there is only one,

To yourself neither one is real,

But I see you inside out.

Impulse

The heart seems to remember how it loved before,

Changing only the face

Of the force

That pumps the pain through the chambers.

A Reel Relationship

I think I'll wait to see the movie of your life,

To find just where I figured in the plot.

Please have them notify me when the film premieres,

I'll try to make it there,

Unless I'm out.

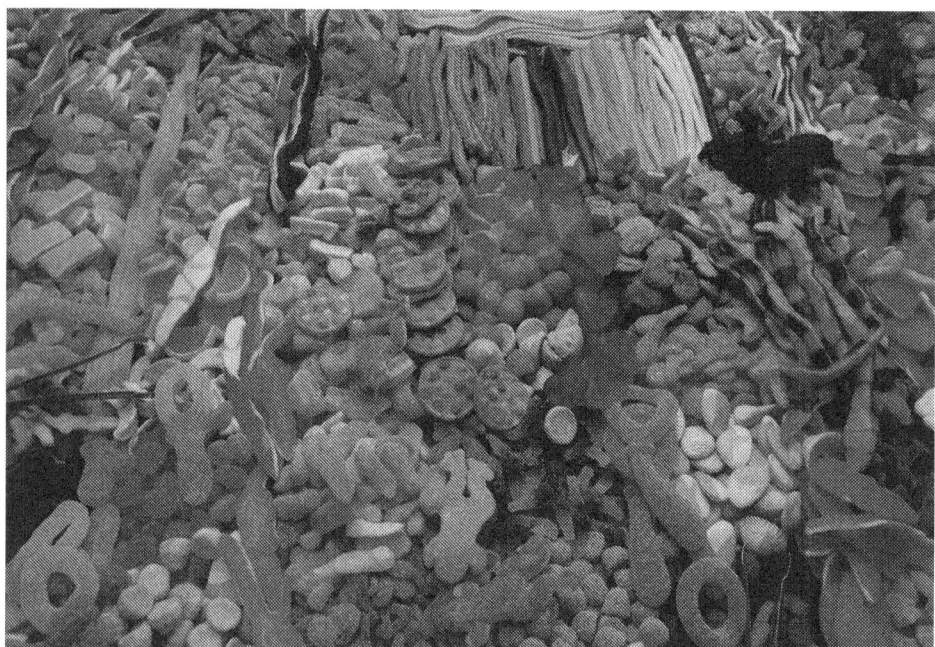

My Candy Dish

My candy dish was full and I

Was eager to invite the hungry people

To take a sample,

Just a piece.

But everybody rushed and grabbed,

Like candy was going out of style.

A few chewed gently,

But others devoured the sweet delights,

And now there is nothing left but

Bittersweet and cream centered memories,

Of what was once a sumptuous array.

Converse

What feeling lie within the eye.

Of two who need each others love,

And somehow do not see the light,

And reaching out can only touch....

a fingertip

A drop of water in the desert,

Whose hearts are dams are bursting peak,

And want to patch the others leak,

But cannot quite contain the flood,

And watch each other drown.

A Sometime Kind of Love Song

I look outside my window, sunbleached scenery in view,

The housefronts melt, the clouds collage,

My memories seep through,

I try to write about the world, To capture something true,

I see your smile, the words go round,

Before I'm done I've somehow found,

My poetry begins and ends with you.

I pass by streets of strangers, friendly faces seem too few,

Their souls disguised, some must be real,

I often wonder who.

I try to write the song I hear, To create something new,

Your voice calls, out, the tune goes round,

And when I'm done I've somehow found,

My melody begins and ends with you.

What do we see, what do we sing?

The books and the music all prove,

We travel our lifetimes in circles that bring,

Everything back to some love.

Warmth and Spire

We ate our breakfast fast and cold,

The morning moments fled,

There wasn't time to let the butter,

Melt on toasted bread,

You always say goodbye,

I wished you'd say godspeed instead,

And I look forward to the heat since you have promised summer.

The pages of my diary remind me of the days,

I've seen you off or said farewell,

A thousand times we've gone our ways,

And through the winter I have seen you,

Like a steeple cast in ice,

I bundle up to fight the chill,

The summer will be nice.

Whatever Little Cells Do When Nobody's Watching Seems Possible

For years she wondered about

Families who lived in Sub-Divisions,

And tried to visualize

How anyone could split themselves apart.

Here a bit of leg,

Here a bit of mind,

Here a bit of arm,

There a bit of heart.

The B.F. Skinner Blues

Well I've been boxed in and locked into patterns I didn't choose,
I have been jaded, frustrated and sold out to pay my dues,
I have been numbered, encumbered, by social security,
I got the B.F. Skinner Blues,
Lord, how I'd hate to lose my freedom and dignity.

I pay my taxes, but lax is my patriotic pride,
I take inflation, corruption and bureaucrats in my stride,
Cause I've been lookin' for shelter, but there ain't no place to hide,
I got the B.F. Skinner Blues,
Lord, how I'd hate to lose my freedom and dignity.

Folks cash in tons of relief checks, the dollar is in distress,
I'll wait in gas lines and breadlines cause Congress won't end this mess,
I wear my WIN pin, cause who loves a loser, but I confess,
I got the B.F. Skinner Blues,
Lord, how I'd hate to lose my freedom and dignity.

I try behaving, I'm slaving, just trying to stay alive,
I keep remembering Darwin and how only the fit survive,
But in the process of struggle, I end up fit to be tied,
I got the B.F. Skinner Blues,
A sinking feeling I'm gonna lose my freedom and dignity.

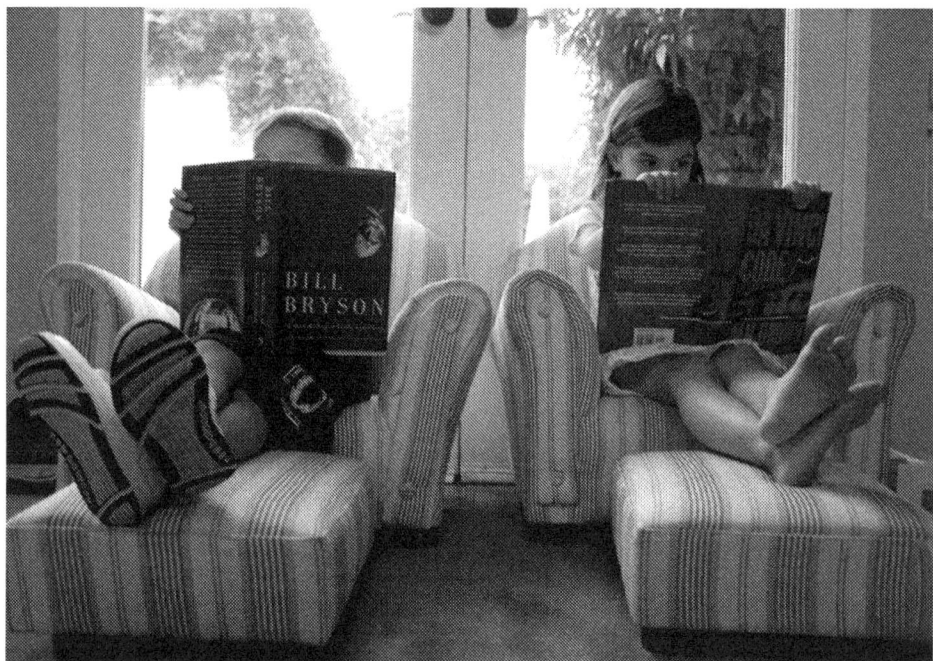

Child Of

Child of the yearning variety,

Sets aside wanting to play,

Reaches inside for reality,

Goes through the motions another day.

Child of the sunshine variety,

Seeks out the pockets of light.

Feeling the glare of mortality,

Walks through the chill of another night.

Child of the living variety,

Breathes in the cinder gray sky,

Chokes on the death wafting in the air,

Gasping, she tries not to cry.

Prisoner of Now and Zenda

Can you separate the threads that twine inside you,

To discover all the patterns time has made ?

Winding down that ball of string that now surrounds you,

To release the type cast mummy that you played.

Have you ever read about the prison riots ?

Are there ever moments when your guard is down ?

When you feel the pounding on the walls around you,

Or clutch for bricks that tumble to the ground.

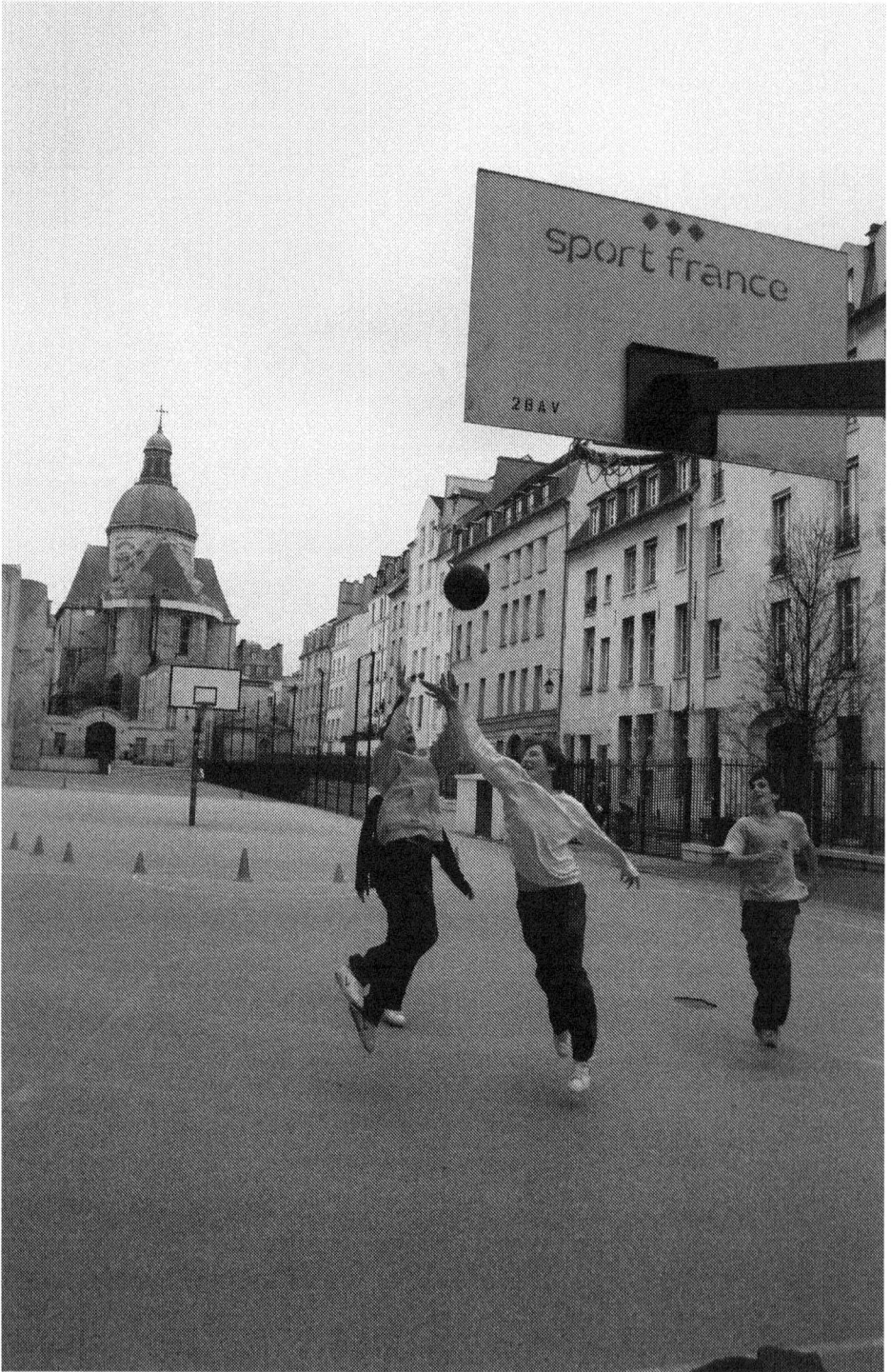

Games

Like I am some monopoly you play,
As if to share meant acting out charades,
Your promises are dominoes,
The matching chains form endless rows,
And ring a round the rosy goes my heart.
I've heard some lovers ask, "What is the score?"
Each day I understand that question more.

My life before you came was solitaire,
My world no bigger than a hopscotch square,
A blind man's bluff, a sometimes sight,
My soul would hide and seek the light,
Freeze tag emotions came to blight my heart.
I've heard some lovers ask "What is the score?"
Each day I understand the question more.

An odds on favorite bet you often hedge,
The scrabble letters spell your precious pledge,
You hold a lot of cards I guess,
In poker games they've killed for less,
I think you're losing, I confess, my heart.
I've heard some lovers ask, "What is the score ?"
Each day I understand the question more.

Inquisition

I keep up my subscription,

To the Scientific American,

With hopes they will someday publish,

The definitive study explaining,

The chemistry of human weakness.

Space Between Us

Memories and dreams,

Row after row

Like picket fencing,

See the slits of daylight dancing,

In the space between us ?

Sleep Talking

What sweet pleasures of the night I take for mine.

Holding your hand and whispering - "good night, god bless,"

And rolling gently in my sleep,

Only to touch you in my travels,

I love the half awakened kisses we exchange,

And sunrise sneaking in.

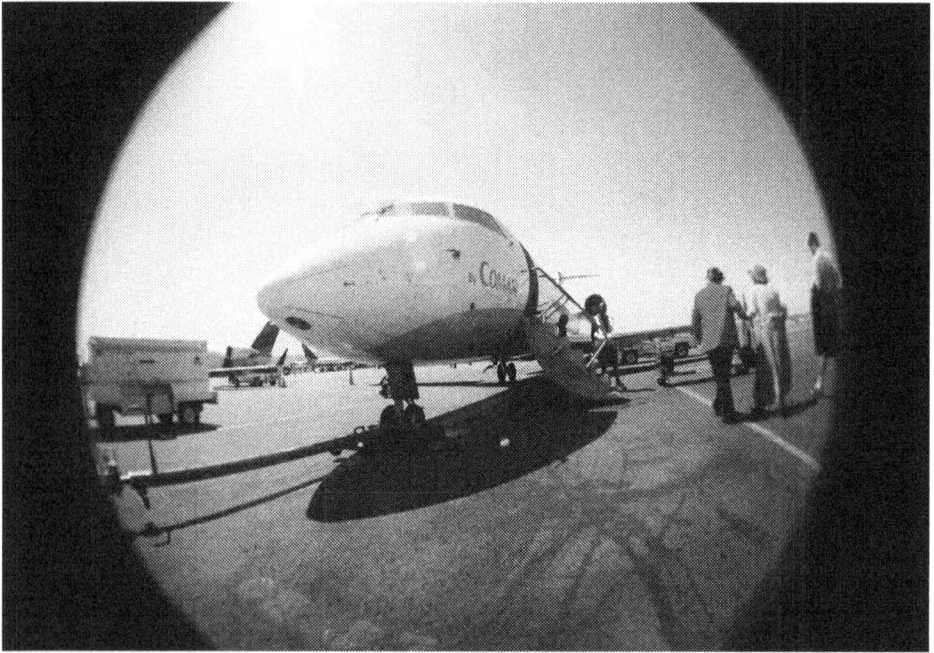

Losing Altitude

It's a ride, another journey out

Coach seat on a flight of fantasy,

To see what life's about.

I know you're flying somewhere,

But never in my direction.

We pass in timezones and in love,

In a maze of missed connections.

It's a ride, another runway down,

Patterned lights like grounded stars,

Another tourist town.

I spend my youth in airport bars,

Learning to travel light,

The cheaper fares are sleeper seats,

They get me through the night.

It's a prayer that goes up every hour,

Pilot to tower, pilot to tower, pilot to tower.

Love Song at 24,000 Feet

I feel like I'm a supersonic angel,

My silver wings keep pushing through the clouds,

I'd like to have you here alone in heaven,

With time away from city streets and crowds,

I'd like to make a bed for us in thin air,

And paint the sky in rainbows, laced with sun,

While all the world went spinning down below us,

I'd bring you peace no earth-bound man has known.

Friends

Friends dropped by,

How lucky can a person be,

They came to tell the truth to me,

To shatter my illusions.

Friends dropped by,

To tell me I have lost again,

A final wound to help me mend,

And leave me in confusion.

Friends dropped by,

To tell me that I should forget,

The promise, payment and the debt,

Then talked about the banker.

Friends dropped by,

One asked that I see what was gone,

Acknowledge that the best man won,

The other asked for silence on,

An evening I'll remember long,

When friends dropped by.

Roll 'Em

You came home and said,

"Let's unwind, let me hold you,

And tell you I love you that way,"

But when I closed my eyes, the walls faded away,

And someone was taking our picture from a helicopter,

The wind was blowing,

whipping honey gold in the first snowfall,

An orchestra was playing our song,

And we laughed when they rolled the credits because

They spelled it wrong.

Hold me fast, angel,

I love being in your movie.

Patchwork People

Look at us now,

What have we become ?

Tattered losses form shreds sewn together with parts that have won,

Pieces of us, we've left behind,

Patches of time.

Fragments of dreams,

Split at the seams,

Pain has ravaged the patterns of youth we were so proud to wear,

Garments with flair, no longer there,

So sadly bare.

Worn at the knees,

Worn at the soul,

Going through life in a quilted disguise that once was whole,

Faded by sun, we've come undone,

Pared to the bone.

Look at us now,

Shabby and shorn,

Cast as waifs in the end with the trappings of finery gone,

Pieces of us, we've left behind,

patches of time.

Momento

Our words when set aside,

No ample epitaph provide,

For what is here inside,

And waiting to be found.

Where nothing else abides,

But gentleness embracing, side by side,

Where secret lovers hide,

What comfort in that fleeting space.

Looking Back

Look back on love,
With smiling eyes,
Give not one thought,
To weeping.
Beauty is priceless
In itself,
And memories worth
Their keeping.

Look back on love,
With silent dreams,
Give not a word
To mar it.
Silence is gold,
But love is more,
And no heart lesser
For it.

Look back on love,
One final time,
See it for what
Was given.
Measure the cost
Of kisses lost,
Tomorrow we go
On living.

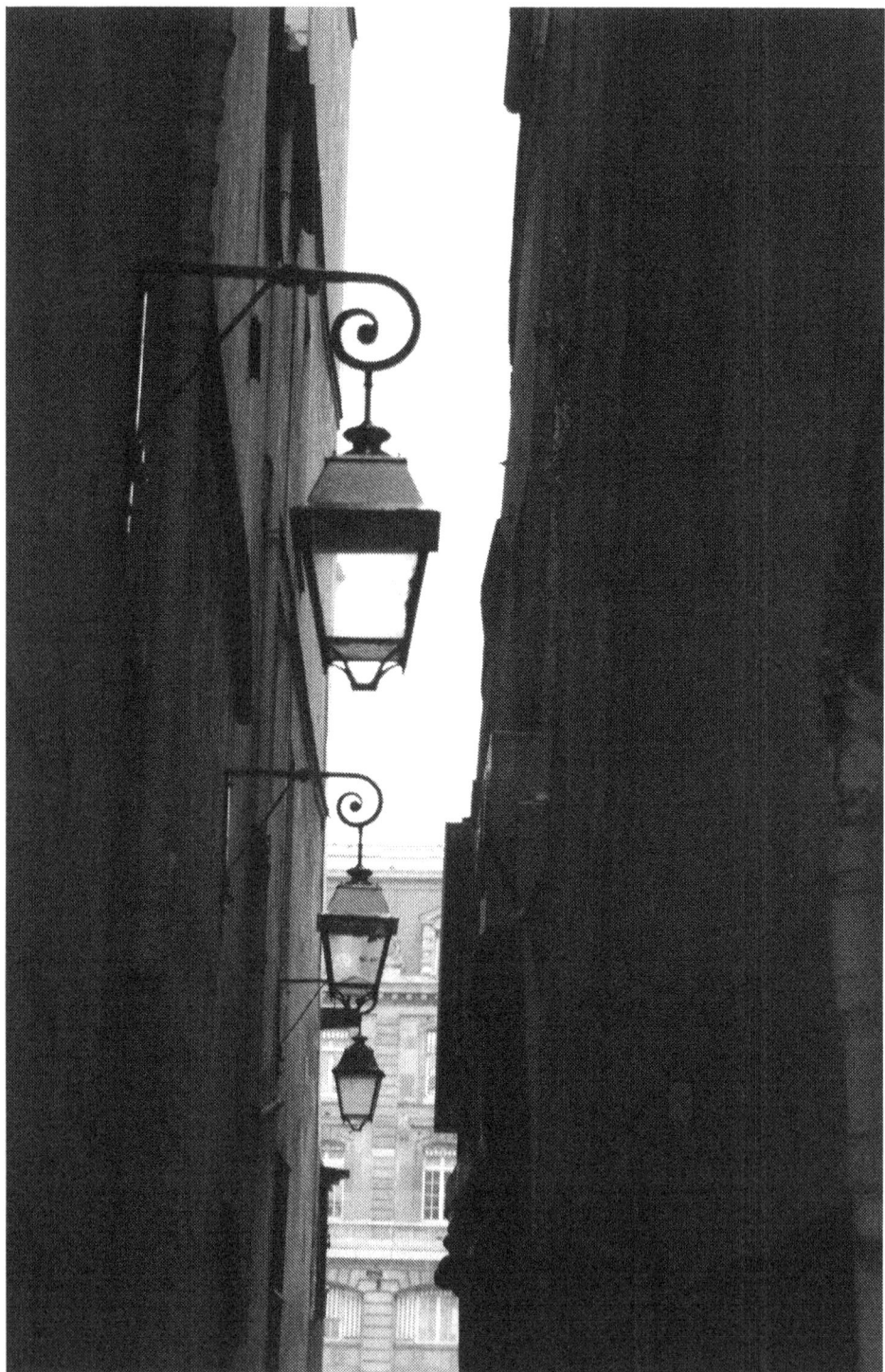

The Keepsake

Keep faith with me and watch the sun,

It shines another hour,

Evening brushes her shoulders up,

And a bell rings out of its tower,

A silent consecration's born,

On the last few moments of light,

Keep faith with me and love me still,

And I'll see you through the night.

Color the Sun with Gray
- A Love Song

Who remembers sunshine before she took her leave,

The echoing of footsteps foreign to my ear concedes,

That he was brief and warm, but misinformed, of what we were to be.

Now sail the coast, the border rocky shaped, claws out to lash the craft,

And if there really was a God I'm sure that he would laugh,

The joke too fragile to survive the stormy sea.

On Your Mercy

See me through soft eyes,

Spared from the harsh world

Of empty dreams.

Keep me from rubbing

Against the sharp edges

Of shattered perfection,

Forgiven.

Incantation of a Weary Traveler

When he had stopped to reckon time,

He saw that he had lived away,

All of his hours now were spent,

Thoughtlessly he had wasted days,

Oh that the calendar were kind,

Age etched upon his face its line,

And wrote his name in dust.

After the walk his pack was shed,

Tools of his trade showed wearing,

Pictures that logged the passageway,

Offered the past for sharing,

Even the words that he had said,

Knew that the voice had gently fled,

How can a stone bear tribute ?

Nursery Rhyme for Troubled Times

There's someone inside you that none of us knows,

Behind all the shadow boxed witty,

The forked tongue that whips us, no mercy will show,

Your castle moat guards all your pretty.

Old Movies

From conscious longings, buried deep,

The feature attraction of my sleep,

Brought back the face of a lover past,

Reuniting star and cast,

The Barrymore of a stage now gone,

Our show closed out of town.

Tunnel Vision

Light falls on the wintered trees,

Purple skies with pink cream rising,

Evening songs no longer please.

Lyrics fail to keep disguising,

Too familiar sung our passions,

Old time tunes we played for nickels,

Take us back to former fashions.

Newer loves show life is fickle.

Take it out and spin it once more,

Circles grow like ivy platters,

Everybody sounds out hollow,

When words are empty what else matters ?

Doodled blueprints of my daydreams,

Super structured memories climb,

Building stories up to heaven,

I'll stand up to see who I am.

Cemetery Ceremonies

We put the dead in their proper places,

Laying to rest the times and spaces,

When life held back the slow return to dust.

We held each other once.

Remember us. ?

We tell our tale and build our monuments,

Paying our way, eternally in debt,

Hoping a friend will love enough to set,

Tears and a proper stone over the plot.

Meet Me at the Station

Sitting there in rows and rows of

Flowing hair beneath their noses,

Sifting out the precious sands of time,

Watching flashes strobe before,

Their open minds, the open door,

Was pouring out the children in a line.

This man's visions, odd distortions,

Colors meshing loom before us,

Birth is paid in full at lover's cost,

Strike the harp and join the passion,

Create beauty in your fashion

Remember he who hesitates is lost.

Go on, grow on,

Meet me at the station,

Delve into the seeing eye of art,

Oh my, goodbye,

Meet me at the station,

Everyone is acting out their part.

Puck's Sea Chanty

I've seen you now from coast to coast,

And caught your sailor's smile before,

With no home port to call you back,

A gentle splash of sea on rock,

I've felt you kiss my shore.

To each a touch, a word to all,

I watch your senses ebb and flow,

As if some secret moon had reign,

To swell a wave of inner pain

That none of us can know.

You pour like tides and spill your soul,

In rippled crescents on the beach,

A pattern mystically unfolds,

Each from a different view beholds,

The rhythms that you teach.

Puck and the Poet

Puck felt the toll as the weariness whirled him,

Lost in the muddle of changes and pains,

Torn between shorelines, old loves tugged the towlines,

His hours filled scorecards with losses and gains,

The poet (in hiding) was lulled by the house game,

Propelled by the backslide of her former fames,

Cocooned in the twilight, her memories were highlights,

The present regrettably still and mundane.

Then Puck touched the poet,

She touched in return,

There was some understanding,

And chemical burn.

Going Home in Pieces

Call for the caskets,

One each for the arms, legs, torso and head,

I am going home in pieces,

Slightly dead.

Call for pallbearers,

One each for the years since I was born,

I am going home in pieces,

To be mourned.

Philosopher

He spends

Hours on end,

Watching for

Metaphors,

Similes and old friends.

Keeps his soul,

In a sack,

Ties it up,

Double knot,

Tossed upon

His bent back.

Terry's Encouragement #2

You are a cup that brims with fire,

Your are a torch that sears the sky,

Breathe to give kindling to the burning,

You are a flame that must not die.

Shine like you meant to fill the heavens,

Love like a twilight's gentle haze,

Roar like thunder when your joy is threatened,

Inside your heart all seasons rage.

Give your own beauty to a landscape,

You choose the colors, dark and light,

You are, alone, the master strokesman,

Painting the portrait of your life.

Tug of War and Peace

Awake - we are in the dream.

Asleep - in the deep recesses of reality,

Between - in the ocean of the mind,

All directions open and in rhythm with the times.

Behind the doors, dark and light we comprise,

Inside - the monsters and the visions,

Within - the monsters and the gods.

Together - we are the fullness and the promise,

Together - we are the strongest and weakest links,

Together - we are one and complete,

Together - we are the whole wave,

But we are also the riptide.

We can pull each other to shore,

We can pull each other out to sea.

What story do we write with passing time,

With distance and experience combined,

Two pools of cosmic dust in search of form,

We are each others shelter, yet the storm.

I am within your soul, but still alone,

You are every cell within me, yet a stone,

We touch with warmth and hardness as we grasp,

For something in ourselves as our lives pass.

Traveling On

Been thinking about this morning,
I know I was unkind,
But lately there are many things,
That keep preying on my mind.
I feel lost inside myself again,
I've got to find the road I'm on,
And I'd leave a forwarding address,
But I don't know where I've gone.
I keep looking beyond the next bend,
For a friendly glimpse of home,
But here scenery gets more alien,
The farther I seem to roam.
There are streets that look like Christmas gardens,
Many doors that only take you out,
There are portraits over the mantelpieces,
Of the strangers that I see about.
I've run down an inch of leather,
Walking off to see the sights
And I send postcards and pleasure verses,
Written softly by my candle's light.
When the mail comes in each morning,
I paste the pictures where I've been,
Together, and I keep on searching,
For a piece of my life again.

The Empty Sonnets

I watched as pink clouds swirled their way toward my eyes,
And wondered where you were beneath the endless skies,
I spoke your name with aching lips,
The longing seared the fingertips,
That bordered empty arms.

That part of me that goes about the pantomime,
That walks the patterned, scheduled paths like someone blind,
I see ahead, but past and through,
Transplanting images of you,
On every empty scene.

The darkness starts my sentence into solitude,
I whisper all my longings, if you only knew,
My memory reaches out in sleep,
and touches silhouettes of peace,
Inside an empty dream.

I curse this void of lost delights and deep despair,
Without you I am just pretending life is real,
There is no measure I can name,
That speaks enough to call this pain,
Out of my empty heart.

Journal Entry

Remember the day we tracked the black squirrel's journey ?

Cresting his underbelly on a drift of snow ?

Spiraling up the aged face of that distinguished old tree ?

Life is an instinct to all, save the poets,

Among God's children.

Growing Pains

Ached inside myself today,

Spasms twitched by body knowings,

Must be growing !

In Honor of Life

To he...

Who I knew all along,

Would come alive some springtime anyway.

Now he'll bloom.

Sweeping up autumn I say,

"Colors change the leaves."

How opposite of me.

I also hold the opinion that

Man changes love.

Some disagree.

But think on it.

Some Men Going Nowhere

Some men like money,

Some drink in bars,

Some watch the stars,

Drive in big cars,

Going nowhere.

Some men are funny,

Some have their pain,

Some have a name,

Trade on their fame,

Going nowhere.

Some men can love you,

Some only try,

Some wonder why,

Time passed them by,

Going nowhere.

Reverie

Bared again,

The self same soul,

Sorrow bent, youth spent,

Heart emptied, love went,

Mirror image, torn, rent,

New gospel's word sent,

Out of heaven,

Out of heaven.

Light rain, windowpane,

Sunday morning fancy came,

Eyes search, how plain,

The self same soul,

Bared again.

The Reservation

You are the love

That comes awhile and flies,

A sudden squall

Before the calm good byes,

A pen that spares

Its precious ink inside,

Open pages

Of other people's lives.

Erratum

Who is love ?

That I have mistaken his identity bids query.

I knew.

At least I thought I did.

I stand corrected.

Summation

Two penny soapbox,

Let off steam,

Imitation heroes,

Phony dreams,

Bargain basement values,

Cut rate lies,

Crocodile tears fall,

Honor dies.

Rambling

Soft pink harbors through the gray,

Children lost in fantasy,

Stray the cobbled paths to middle ground,

Tapping stones toward and end,

One night playmates, next day friends,

Shadows sleep by candle, shutters down.

Will you wander on with me?

Make a fool of destiny,

Fast forgetting patterns of the game,

Take me now for time will pass,

Fond, remembering the lass,

Generous...he won't recall her name.

New Edition

It was rumored

That he cared more than a farthing.

The words escaped a fluent tongue,

What in those eyes was harboring ?

A new edition

Was put out for the lending,

Reality's a pretty penny now,

No use pretending.

The Heartbeat Waltz

Has he heard my heart crying,

As one season fades, does he know that I'm lying,

In our game of charades, does he listen to heartbeats,

Counting the pulses,

In time to the waltzes,

Whose tempos were somewhat more bright

Then tonight.

When my sleep in entangled

And peace is not won,

Does he ever remember

The things we have done ?

Can he feel how my heartbeats,

Sounds gently given

A ballad-like rhythm,

In songs that were somewhat more gay

Then today.

Dear Me How Curious

Echoes of a small ovation

Linger in the wings at dusk,

Tears for lines that they forgot,

To remember, ever after,

Nervous laughter,

Wilted yellow roses,

Rapture,

And a star upon a door,

Used playbills stack

Commemorating

Old actors,

Old stages,

Old pages in their lives,

Once excited,

Once delighted,

Certain curtains down paraded,

Past the inner eyes of daydreams,

Trembling at the sight.

Facing It

We touch the faces of strangers

Until we begin to feel

The outline of a friend,

Slow in the beginning,

Tender in the end,

When smiles can be drawn from memories,

On canvases of solitary reveries,

And knowing all of human imperfection,

The heart still finds reason to love.

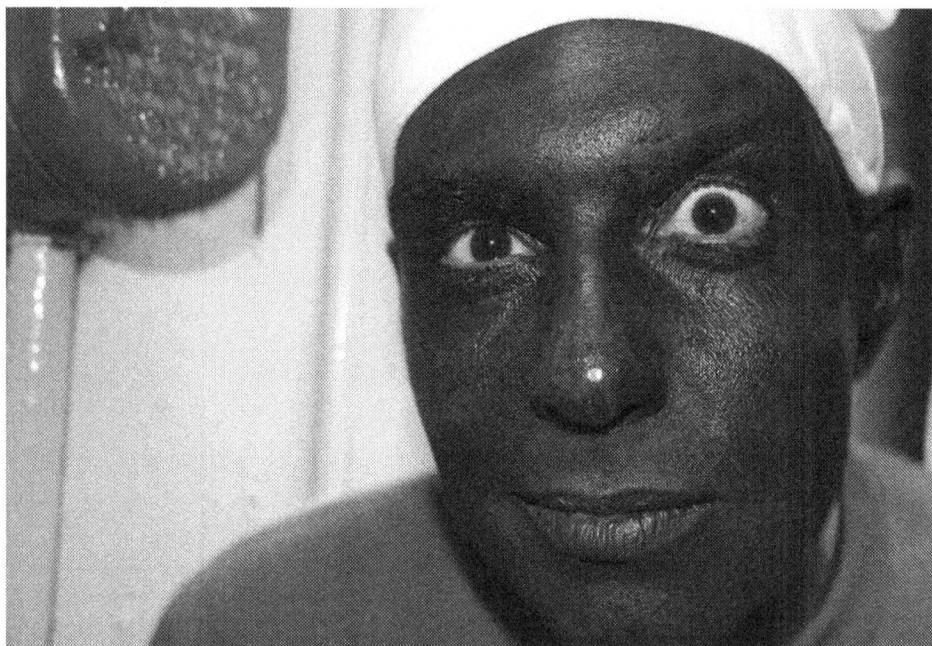

The Carnival of Madness

At the carnival of madness,

All must enter in the doorway,

Save the tall man push reality away,

In the center ring the lion, in his cage, is taming people,

See the glory and the spectacle arrayed,

With the freakish crowd assembled

There to stare at all the normal,

The tall man finds the paradox reversed.

On the trapeze swings the balance between infancy and death,

And the ringmaster is waiting for the worst.

On this solitary resting place

For children of the sawdust,

The tall man of the side show gazes down.

Where underneath a canvas tent, a three ring circus rages,

The face of life is painted on a clown.

Hot Fudge Sundaes Anyone?

The children are having affairs today,

Out in the sun will ruin,

Beware of the mother who lets you play,

Never before concurrent!

Over the barrel we grin and sigh,

Bouncing the knee one wearies,

It matters and yet it matters not,

Up til the end one hurries.

Left Out in the Light

Emanating from,

But not precisely,

Out for the fun of sport, and doing nicely.

Warmth

on a circle,

out of the hutch and pinned to life...

Peek-aboo...somebody new...

Peach fuzz basking,

Left out in the light.

Prophet Bound

I just got back

From many years,

Of traveling

In tiny spheres,

The world is not as round as roads are tred.

The people never saw me there,

But with their burdens and their cares,

I couldn't tell the living from the dead.

The oceans cleft,

The tides were rift,

My soul was lost,

My heart adrift,

My body at the mercy of the storm.

The sun was set

Behind a hand,

Whose fingers reached

To touch the land,

The agony of life was taking form.

The news came out

In boldface lies,

That headlined

Twisted truth disguised,

Who sees the mirror from the other side ?

The deaf could hear,

The blind could see,

The masquerade,

The fallacies,

A mountain seldom finds a place to hide.

I'm packing up my bag again,

My feet will walk, my lips defend,

The right of man to cross and break a line,

When dynasties their evil cease,

The injured hawk will seek the peace,

The wounds he licks will lick him back in time.

Canticles

I lay on the bed

for that's where we have been

and

where dreams of holding your hand,

our fingers forever entwined,

the touch of love,

beneath the covers haunt.

I take out the bits

of paper written in the past

and

where the words of giving your heart,

our souls forever entwined,

a gift of love,

between the pages haunt.

You are the sacred festival.

There is the celebration of emptying out

your cigarette ashes,

And pausing to worship the places you sat,

the quoting of you like some absolute gospel,

The religion built around the uttering of your name.

I light a lot of candles now.

Fragrances drift,

Apple blossom and raspberries drip,

Cascading down the sherry bottle.

There are still traces of the last we burned together.

The flicker hypnotizes while dancing

And all of your memories are shadowed against the night.

I light a lot of candles now,

Hoping perhaps you'll find your way home.

Feelings

If feelings were a piece of clay,

I'd mold the shape to fit my soul,

And putty in the cracks and flaws,

The hollow spots where love seeps out,

Instead of keeping nothing in.

Tis better to have loved and lost,

They say without a second thought,

But I say NO.

It all depends on what you've lost,

And who you've loved,

And why you let it go.

What Persists (Restated)

Celebrate life, they said,

Fill the transparent cup to invite

The passing of lips.

This is the ceremonial upheaval,

The instantaneous desire to kiss

the foreheads

of those you might only say hello to otherwise,

Otherwise...

the vacuum persists.

We are a block of stone, they said,

Life is what sculpt us, takes the blows,

Fashions the soul, the chips, the chips,

These are what form the art we feel,

The tears we cry and laughter, stolen laughter.

The insatiable urge to kiss

the eyes

of those you might not have held in awe otherwise,

Otherwise...

the granite persists.

This Vexation

Pull up the stakes

That tie you down, my friend,

Compassion makes the load a little lighter,

And the men much better men.

The Lovers - Two Duets

And if she was love,

Why the vacant stare and lifeless air ?

And if he was love,

Why the trembling hands and dying trees ?

And if she was love,

Why the night spent quivering alone ?

And if he was love,

Of course he'd come to bring her home.

And if she was love,

Why a portrait of their backs and hate ?

And if he was love,

Why the violent judgments and sudden peace ?

And if she was love,

Why the quick defense and pain deny ?

And if he was love,

Of course he'd cry.

Haiku

single teardrop fell
trickled down and eased the pain,
sorrow lingered on.

pudgy pink and softness
rounded, twitched with fascination,
God's creation - baby toes.

delicate to touch
and bruises leave a history
of many fingers.

instants fled swiftly,
time forbade the nodding of
an old weary head.

wisdom is not mine,

not when my thoughts are jumbled

into such strange art.

love as candles melt

is soft and warm forming shapes,

molded into hearts.

even if a branch

breaks off and curses nature,

the tree does not die.

neither wild animals

nor the fancies of poets

can ever be tamed.

The Banquet

Learning

The key to treasures vast,

Tomorrow is locked

Inside the past.

Kindling lights

The human pyre,

Man thinks

And sets the world on fire.

Knowledge to man is,

As it ought,

Progress - digested food

For thought.

Man without mind

Is as the least,

Here lies the banquet,

Come and feast.

The Streetlamp Poem

There once upon a night stood we,

As Shakespeare deigned it perfectly,

Two lovers found atop a balcony.

Who bled their loneliness atwain,

Braiding strands of happiness and pain,

Two losses now an interwoven gain.

No courage asked of cowards who would run,

No judgment asked for what in days was done,

Two crossroads destinations end as one.

Syllabus

Dwindling into vats of letters,

Empty words all melt together,

Syllables dismember slowly,

Consonants are dissipated,

Vowels dissolve and

Such related parts

Of speech are

Segregated.

Fallacies

settle in

the pot.

Truth

forms

resi

due

on

the

top.

Free Lunch

Come to my table,

Nature has been good to me this season,

The pantry is overflowing.

Not to invite you in

Would leave the nourishment to spoil.

It's there for the taking,

A harvest between friends.

Bring what you can or care to,

Come as you are, hungry.

Let us succor the same tastes on our tongues

And savor the knowledge,

That this is but one of the experiences

Life has for us to share.

The Dare

The one legged man,

With his battered crutch,

Faced down the weary

Rutted trail.

Keeping his shoulder

Blade

Unhunched...

Pondering whether

To take the dare.

The Last Will and Testament of a Dying Butterfly

Day filtered down,

On to a garden's member,

One butterfly,

Flew into her December.

Tears were shed once,

once for a final penance,

Life was her only foe,

Death her menace.

Countenance has passed,

Divinity ended,

Somewhere

Where once a butterfly descended.

Bitterweed

Love grows inside you,

In a briar patch,

Where hurt is rooted deep,

And tendrils close around your jaded spirit,

Choking your life away.

Up to the Door

Up to the door

She came to stay,

And waved goodbye

To yesterday,

And all the games

That children play,

And said hello

To love.

"I Might Be Driven To Sell Your Love For Peace."

(based on a line from Edna St. Vincent Millay)

Tonight the feathered pillows feel like stone,

And every sound a thousand beating drums,

In darkness there is shelter to forget,

And sleep against all dreams, if it would come.

Tonight your head may rest and not alone,

And I begin to pray against my fears,

If only there were stars that prophesied.

And moon enough to see the truth from here.

The day brings urchin vendors to the street,

And I will take my torment in quatrain,

And bargain passing strangers for my poems,

To buy some peace by selling off the pain.

Soundings

Inside of you I hear

Two very separate chambers of the same heart,

Beating against each other,

Pounding fear and love together

Like a frantic native drum.

Cacophonies of self confusion,

Doubts and pleas in alternating rhythms,

With noise enough to deafen the soul,

To the sound of its own music.

After the Rush

If only you'd stop running,

Running to be caught in time,

Snagged by the stories you told,

About yourself and love.

If only you'd stop trying,

Trying to be there at last,

Tripped by the gaps between lies,

About yourself and love.

If only you'd start living,

Living as if it was real,

Blessed by the people you let

Close to yourself and love.

Superstars

Heavenly bodies,

Supernovas,

Two lives that touch

With the frequency of passing comets.

Momentary suns

In an infinite blackness,

Lighting the corners

Of transitory hearts.

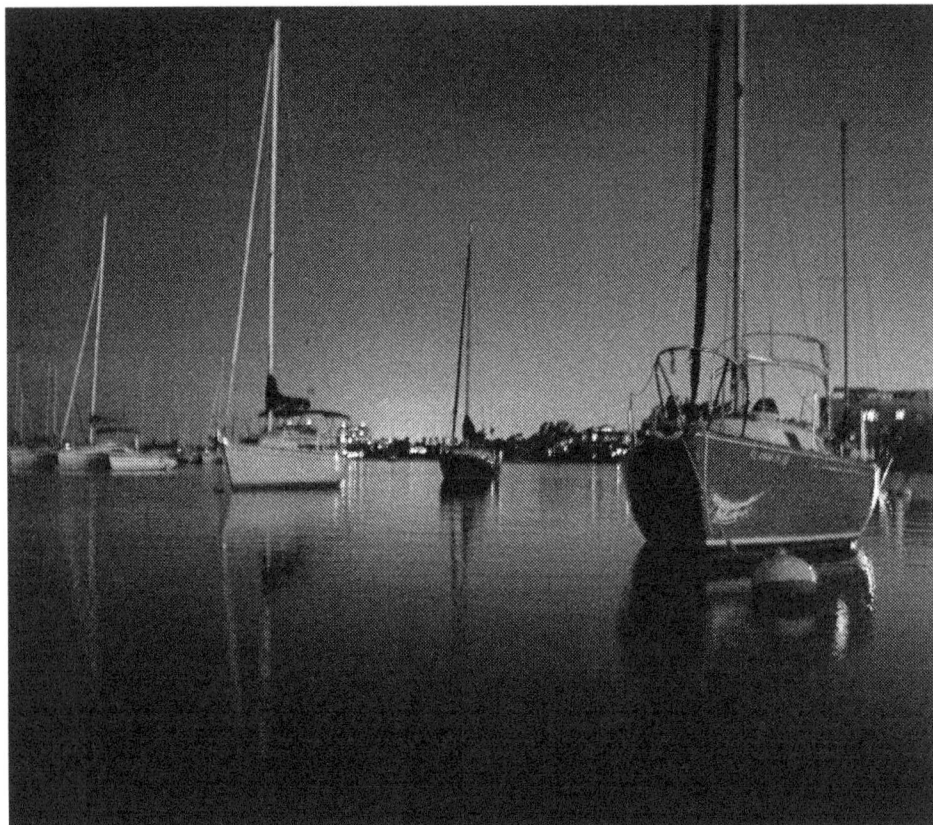

The Last of the Great Romantics

The last of the great romantics,

Is plotting his escape by sea,

Wind powered,

To where he wants to be.

Meanwhile,

The soul survives,

Not looking out the window,

Except to check the tides.

Ava's Song

When I am rich enough to be idle,

I plan to re-invest

In toys,

For the children,

Lost in action,

Inside the bodies of

My aging friends.

"DO YOU HEAR THAT ?
THE CYMBALS AGAIN,"
HE SAID.
"HOPE"

www.ingramcontent.com/pod-product-compliance
Lightning Source LLC
Chambersburg PA
CBHW032059080426
42733CB00006B/347